Just Joking
SPORTS

NATIONAL
GEOGRAPHIC
KiDS

Just Joking SPORTS

Joe Funk

NATIONAL GEOGRAPHIC
WASHINGTON, D.C.

A skunk can spray a target from up to 12 feet (3.6 m) away.

5

Super Cool Sports

SPECTACULAR SPORT:

Sumo wrestling

LOCATION: Japan

SURPRISING STATS:

Sumo wrestling dates back to over 1,500 years ago and originally began as a festival performance meant to entertain the gods. Today, sumo wrestling is the national sport of Japan and regularly sells out the largest arenas throughout the island nation. Modern sumo wrestlers, called Rikishi, still observe many of the sport's traditions in pre-bout ceremonies in which they perform moves such as stomping to ward off demons or throwing salt to purify the wrestling ring. The wrestlers, who weigh an average of 330 pounds (150 kg), then begin the bout by grappling with their hands. Sumo wrestlers are among the biggest celebrities in Japan, are revered by fans, and are even supported by their training quarters into retirement.

To maintain their weight, sumo wrestlers eat a Japanese stew called chankonabe.

A sumo wrestler's traditional hairstyle, known as the topknot, was the hairstyle of Japan's Edo period.

Q What did one fan say to the other fan?

A Nothing, they just did the wave.

Say this fast three times:

Trudy tooted in her suit on the luge tube.

Q What's the least expensive thing at a basketball game?

A A free throw.

Q What is a hornet's favorite sport?

A Rug-bee.

Q Why was the dog banned from the football game?

A For unnecessary ruff-ness.

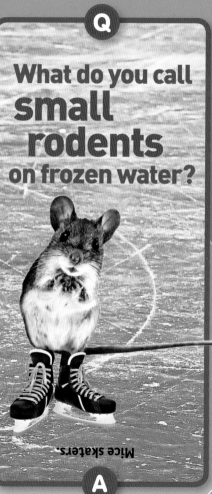

Q What do you call **small rodents** on frozen water?

A Mice skaters.

10

ANIMAL:
African elephant

NAME: **Elise**

FAVORITE SPORT:
Squash

FAVORITE SPORTS PLAY:
Seeing a snowboarder stomp a landing

LOSING NEVER BOTHERS ME ... I HAVE THICK SKIN!

Fierce FANS

Say this fast three times:

Sue knew the gnu scored two.

Q What do basketball players like to do most with cookies and doughnuts?

Dunk 'em!

A

Why was the fisherman also such a good basketball player?

Q

He already had a great hook shot.

A

Sports TALK

IF I WERE A GIRAFFE, I'D HAVE WON THIS RACE!

HA! HA! HA! HA! HA!

The toucan's impressive bill is mainly for show.

KNOCK, KNOCK.

Who's there?
Toucan.
Toucan who?
Toucan play at that game!

13

"You said
go long—
is this far
enough?"

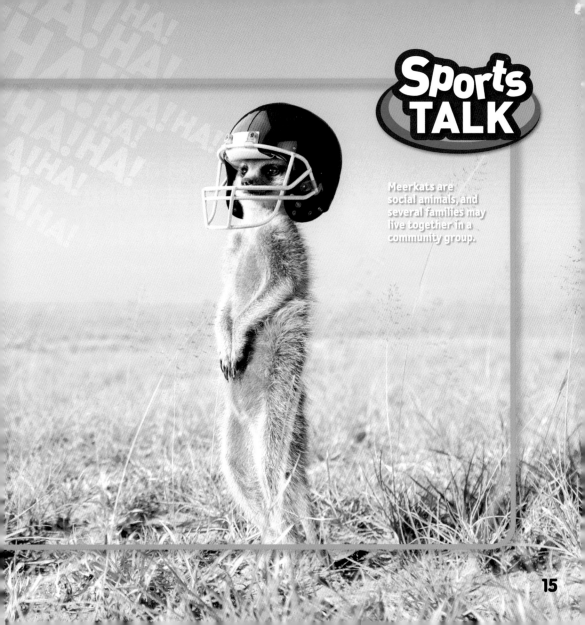

Sports TALK

Meerkats are social animals, and several families may live together in a community group.

Q

What was the hockey player's **favorite childhood game?**

Puck, puck, goose.

A

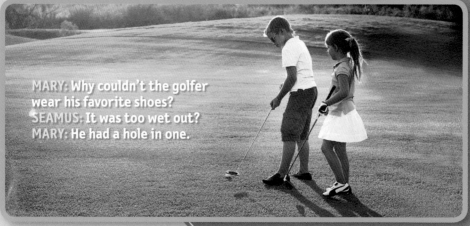

MARY: Why couldn't the golfer wear his favorite shoes?
SEAMUS: It was too wet out?
MARY: He had a hole in one.

Why couldn't the **porcupine** ever win a race?

Q

She was just too pokey.

A

17

Q What two sports does a baker like most?

A Basketball for the pick-and-rolls; motorsports for the victory doughnuts.

SportsTALK

ISN'T "SMASHMOUTH" A TERM USED IN AMERICAN FOOTBALL?

Q How did the **chef** kick the soccer ball?

A She drilled it with her pota-toe.

Q Why did the sailing team cancel the race?

A They were sure it was rigged.

KNOCK, KNOCK.

Who's there?
Whale.
Whale who?
Whale you were away getting nachos, our team scored!

Belugas communicate through clicks, whistles, and clangs.

19

Female blue marlins can weigh nearly 2,000 pounds (907 kg)!

Q What is a vegetable's favorite **martial art?**

A Carrot-e.

Q What is a ghost's favorite position?

A Ghoul-keeper.

Like people, many mammals sneeze to eject irritants from their nose.

Say this fast three times:

Trish twisted to whisk the discus.

EUGENE: Did you hear about the bowler who went to jail?
CATHERINE: No, what happened?
EUGENE: She said she was framed.
CATHERINE: And who does she think framed her?
EUGENE: She couldn't pin it down.

Q What skateboarding maneuver would a platypus like most?

A Goofyfoot.

Q Why was Frosty so good at pitching?

A He always threw a snow-hitter.

Fierce FANS

WHO NEEDS LEGS?

ANIMAL: **Python**
NAME: **Pedro**
FAVORITE SPORT: **Curling**
FAVORITE SPORTS PLAY:
Seeing the squeeze play in baseball

SPECTACULAR SPORT:

Competitive eating

LOCATION: Coney Island, NY, U.S.A.

SURPRISING STATS:

According to legend, on July 4, 1916, four immigrants to America decided to settle an argument over who was most patriotic by holding a hot dog eating contest. This began an annual tradition that continues today in the form of Nathan's Hot Dog Eating Contest, founded that same year. Today, contestants of the gorge fest are given 10 minutes to eat as many hot dogs as they are able. They are allowed water and condiments, and the winner receives a prized bejeweled belt. Winners also get their names entered into the Nathan's Hall of Fame.

The 2016 winner holds the current record for eating 73.5 hot dogs and buns in 10 minutes.

Contestants can receive penalty cards for "messy eating."

Super Cool
★★
Sports

Why do zombies like watching hockey and football?

A They can't get enough of the faceoffs and handoffs.

Q

What sort of sports event does a cat admire most?

A A purr-fect game.

Q

Where would a **school of fish** sit at a game?

A The student section.

ZAM

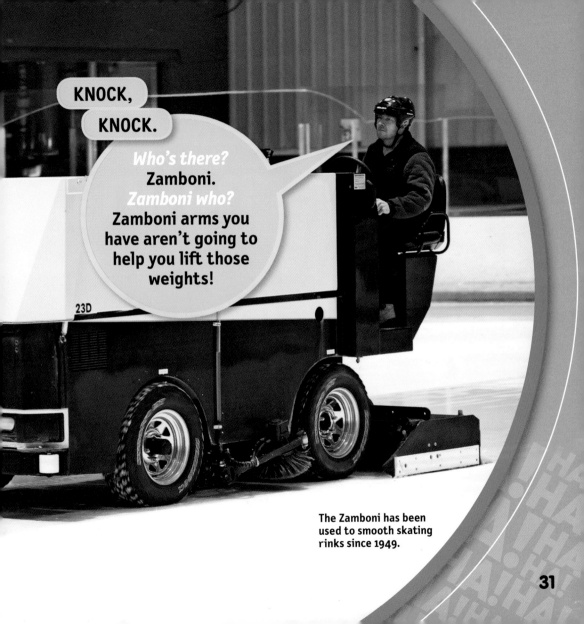

The Zamboni has been used to smooth skating rinks since 1949.

Q

What type of game does a hibernating bear hope for?

A snoozer.

A

Q What type of game would a **breaching whale** root for?

A A blowout!

Q What type of game would a king and queen root for?

A A reign-out!

33

Q How does a swordsman protect his lunch?

A With fencing.

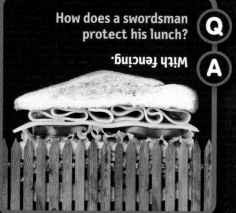

Say this fast three times:

Brenda the batter bunted better.

Q Why are **vampires** afraid of **volleyball** games?

A They don't like all the spikes.

Q How did the track star overcome her fear of hurdles?

A She just got over it.

Q Why was the horse sad?

A He was afraid he couldn't race any-mare.

Q What did the coach yell to the marsupial heading for the end zone?

A "Koala way!"

36

KNOCK, KNOCK.

Who's there?
Defense.
Defense who?
Defense has a hole in it, that's how I got in.

Soccer is thought to have originated in China around the second century B.C.

37

ANIMAL: Tortoise
NAME: Terry
FAVORITE SPORT: Football
FAVORITE SPORTS PLAY: The long snappers

SPEED IS OVERRATED!

Fierce
FANS

Q What is the hardest thing about learning to **figure skate?**

A The ice.

Q Why didn't the dog want to play catch?

A She was a boxer.

KNOCK, KNOCK.

Who's there?
Ostrich.
Ostrich who?
Ostrich before I go on a run, don't you?

The world's largest bird can stand up to nine feet (2.7 m) tall.

JOEY: Why was the champion RC pilot's victory speech cut short?
JANEY: He tooted?
JOEY: He kept droning on and on.

Sports TALK

SORRY FOR THE DRONE PUN. IT'S NOT EVEN REMOTELY FUNNY.

Q What is a **lumberjack's favorite sushi?**

A The log roll.

KNOCK, KNOCK.

Who's there?
Gorilla.
Gorilla who?
Race cars sure can gorilla fast.

There are only several hundred mountain gorillas remaining on Earth.

Q Why were the **ducks ejected** from the game?

A Too many fowls.

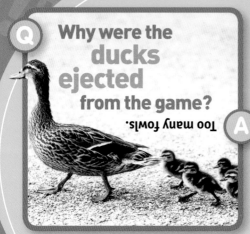

Q Why shouldn't babies play point guard?

A They dribble way too much.

Q What did the insect do after getting hit by a pitch?

A Made a beeline for first base.

TONGUE TWISTER!

Say this fast three times:

Susan tooted a vuvuzela to keep her team from losing.

Q Why was the singer great at **baseball?**

A She had perfect pitch.

DESHAWN: What did the boxer do when he saw Dracula?
LUCY: Ran away?
DESHAWN: He fell down for the count.

CAN I PLEASE BE THE UMPIRE? I'LL KEEP HOME PLATE LICKED CLEAN!

Sports TALK

49

The world record for the largest kite ever flown belongs to a kite more than 83 feet (25 m) long and 131 feet (40 m) wide.

Super Cool ★★
★ Sports

SPECTACULAR SPORT:
Competitive kite flying

LOCATION: Worldwide

SURPRISING STATS:

Imagine figure skating in the air, and you'll probably be picturing something close to competitive kite flying. In Japan, the Hamamatsu Kite Flying Festival is more than 450 years old and features traditionally decorated kites more than 11 feet (3.5 m) long. The festival historically featured kite battles, but over time came to symbolize the births of a local lord's children. At newer competitions and festivals around the world, such as France's World Sport Kite Championship, competitors are judged on their ability to lead the kite through a series of figures or to direct the kite in an artistic musical interpretive dance.

The earliest kites might have been flown in China more than 2,800 years ago.

On May 5th in Japan, it is traditional to fly carp-shaped streamers known as *koinobori*.

51

What do rhinos like to see most in baseball?

Q

When the infield throws it around the horn.

A

"Why did the horse need to stretch a little extra in winter?"

A He was so colt.

Say this fast three times:

The speedy shortstop slid safely.

What was the **pirate's** favorite baseball stat?

An ARRBI.

Q What's the first thing a football player does before fishing?

A He tackles the bait.

The Malay word "orangutan" means "person of the forest."

KNOCK,

KNOCK.

Who's there?
Swish.
Swish who?
Swish your shoes, they're on the wrong feet.

55

What did **Saturn** get when it won the **tournament?**

A championship ring.

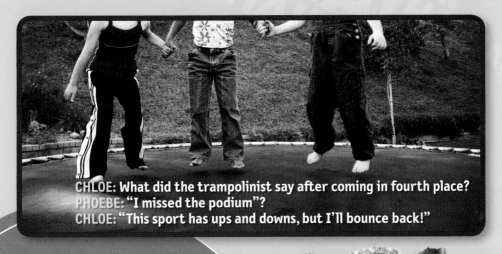

CHLOE: What did the trampolinist say after coming in fourth place?
PHOEBE: "I missed the podium"?
CHLOE: "This sport has ups and downs, but I'll bounce back!"

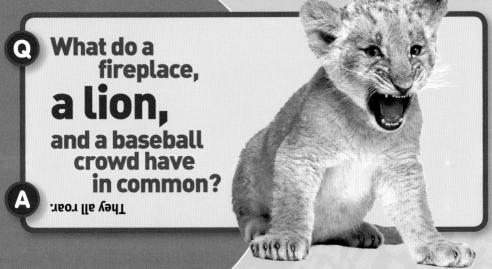

Q What do a fireplace, **a lion,** and a baseball crowd have in common?

A They all roar.

57

Though they live mostly in water, hippos come on land to feed at night, and they can match a human's speed for short distances.

Q What would you serve to others that you can **never eat** yourself?

A A tennis ball.

Q Why can't dogs win dance competitions?

A They have two left feet.

Pelicans use their elastic throat pouches to catch fish.

KNOCK, KNOCK.

Who's there?
Buoy.
Buoy who?
Buoy, that was a great boat race!

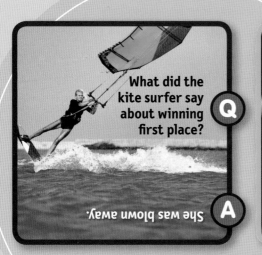

Q What did the kite surfer say about winning first place?

A She was blown away.

Say this fast three times:

Dot swished a shot from that spot.

Q How did the Scottie dog feel about having to race a greyhound?

A He was terrier-fed.

Q Why wasn't the chicken good at pitching?

A He kept bawk-ing.

NINA: What did the sneakers say to the race car?
JACKSON: Sneakers can talk?
NINA: "You drive, I'll go on foot."

KNOCK, KNOCK.

Who's there?
Roblox.
Roblox who?
Roblox the defenders, so you can run for a score!

64

Q What do you call a pig who won't pass the basketball?

A A ball hog.

Q What award did **Chewbacca** win after his **first year of baseball?**

A Wookiee of the Year.

I'M GLAD I DON'T USE THESE TINY HANDS TO EAT!

ANIMAL:
Tyrannosaurus rex

NAME: Tony

FAVORITE SPORT:
Any sport that doesn't require him to use his tiny arms

FAVORITE SPORTS PLAY: Pie-eating competitions

Fierce FANS

What do you get
when you cross a quarterback
with a three-line poem?

A hike-u.

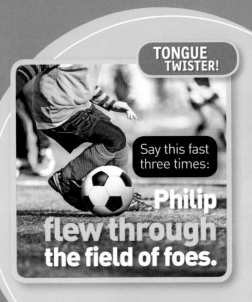

Say this fast three times:

Philip flew through the field of foes.

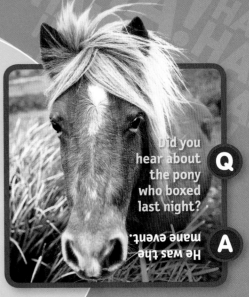

Q Did you hear about the pony who boxed last night?

A He was the mane event.

Q Why aren't ostriches any good at volley-ball?

A They always have their head in the sand.

Q How do surfers get clean after a tournament?

A They wash up on shore.

70

A treasure hunter's favorite sports teams:

- **Golden State Warriors**
- **San Francisco 49ers**
- **Denver Nuggets**
- **Vegas Golden Knights**

SPECTACULAR SPORT:

Palio di Siena

LOCATION: Siena, Italy

SURPRISING STATS:

Often considered the most important event in Siena, Italy, the Palio is a horse race that occurs twice a year to celebrate the Virgin Mary. Each of the 17 districts of the city has a chance to compete in a colorful and frantic mounted horse race around the town's central plaza, the Piazza del Campo. Each district has its own colors, emblems, and flags and takes part in a celebratory costume parade.

Although the first official Palio di Siena took place in 1656, Siena has been home to horse racing since the sixth century.

The emblems of the 17 city districts include a snail, a unicorn, a dragon, a she-wolf, a porcupine, and a goose, among others.

Super Cool ★★
★ Sports

Q Why did the police rush to the softball game?

A Someone was stealing a base.

Q Where do sports teams go for **new** uniforms?

A New Jersey.

74

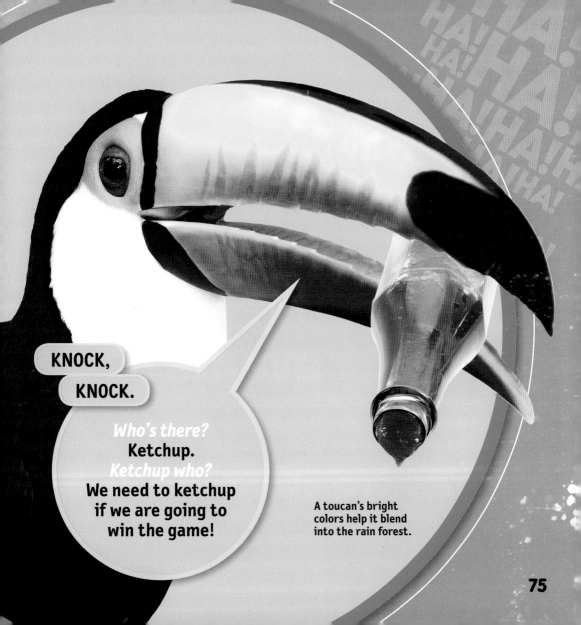

KNOCK,
KNOCK.

Who's there?
Ketchup.
Ketchup who?
We need to ketchup
if we are going to
win the game!

A toucan's bright
colors help it blend
into the rain forest.

75

Q

Why do
sharks
like to watch
competitive eating
events?

They appreciate
a good feeding
frenzy.

A

Q What position is a Dalmatian best suited for in weight lifting?

A Spotter.

Q Why are elephants good at snowboarding?

A They stomp their landings.

Q Why do vampires like to see a long home run in baseball?

A They love to see a good bat flip.

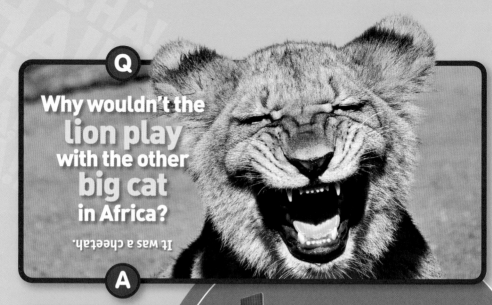

Q

Why wouldn't the **lion play** with the other **big cat** in Africa?

A

It was a cheetah.

Q What's **black and white** and **red** all over?

A A referee with a sunburn.

80

ANIMAL: Vampire bat
NAME: Veronica
FAVORITE SPORT:
Any sport with a timer
FAVORITE SPORTS PLAY:
Watching the winning team bleed the clock

I GO BATTY FOR SPORTS!

Fierce FANS

Q **What kind of dogs make the best cheerleaders?**

A Pom-Pomeranians.

Q **What team do second-string insects play on?**

A The bee team.

83

There are about 400 different breeds of horses.

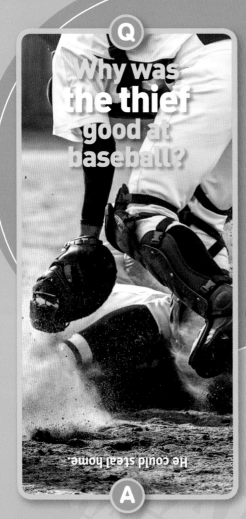

Q Why was the thief good at baseball?

A He could steal home.

Q How did the computer win the eating competition?

A It took a lot of megabytes.

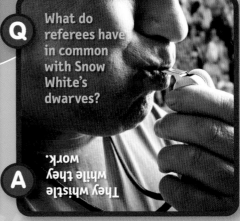

Q What do referees have in common with Snow White's dwarves?

A They whistle while they work.

Q Why are birders attracted to golf?

A Because of all the birdies and eagles.

Q What's a race car driver's favorite snack?

A Doughnuts.

Q What animal do sports teams want **to hear least?**

A Cari-boos!

BOO!

Q Why do frogs go to baseball games?

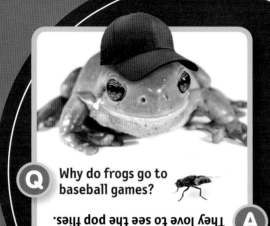

A They love to see the pop flies.

Q Why did the cow wear goggles to the archery match?

A Everyone was aiming for the bull's-eye.

Q Why did the **giraffe** **love** the horse race?

A The winning mount won by a neck.

Q What look might a **skunk give** to a ref who made a **bad call?**

A The stink eye.

Why do lions, tigers, and bears like the last five minutes of a basketball game?

Because of all the paw-ses at the end.

A cowboy's favorite sports teams:

- Chicago Bulls
- San Antonio Spurs
- Denver Broncos
- Indianapolis Colts
- Buffalo Bills
- Dallas Cowboys
- Houston Texans

Like many sports, points are awarded in kung fu and other martial arts.

Super Cool ★★
★Sports

SPECTACULAR SPORT:

The Masai Mara Marathon

LOCATION: Masai Mara National Reserve, Kenya

SURPRISING STATS:

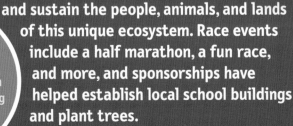

Sports may be fun, but they can also be so much more! Combining amazing athletics and conservation, the Masai Mara Marathon hosts runners from all over the world to help preserve the Masai Mara ecosystem, home to the Maasai people as well as many animals. Started in just the last decade, the race has accomplished the organizer's goals of bringing much needed attention to this stunning habitat, and the proceeds help preserve and sustain the people, animals, and lands of this unique ecosystem. Race events include a half marathon, a fun race, and more, and sponsorships have helped establish local school buildings and plant trees.

Maasai people speak Maa, as well as English and Swahili.

The Maasai people are thought to have originally come from northern Africa along the Nile Valley.

95

Q Why was the **pirate** put in the penalty box?

A For hooking.

Q What sport do elephants play with bugs?

A Squash.

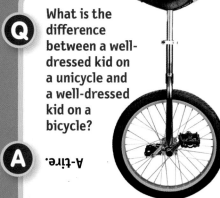

Q What is the difference between a well-dressed kid on a unicycle and a well-dressed kid on a bicycle?

A A-tire.

Sports TALK

I LIKE SOCCER BECAUSE OF ALL THE KICKING!

I BET HUMANS WISH THEY HAD HANDS FOR FEET!

ANIMAL: Ape
NAME: George
FAVORITE SPORT: Handball
FAVORITE SPORTS PLAY: Seeing a coach go bananas

Fierce FANS

A wildebeest migration can involve up to 1.5 million of the animals.

An astronaut's favorite sports teams:

- Phoenix Suns
- Dallas Stars
- Houston Astros
- Houston Rockets

What is a boa constrictor's **favorite play** in baseball? Q

A The squeeze play.

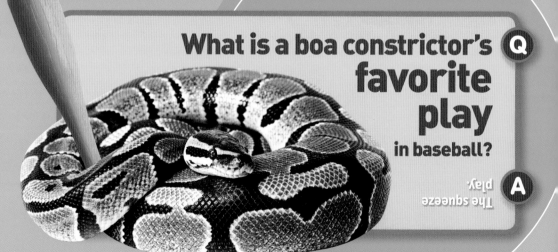

Q Why don't **spiders** like **goalies?**

A They try to stop anything from going in their nets.

101

Q Why don't tennis players go on dates?

A Because love means nothing to them.

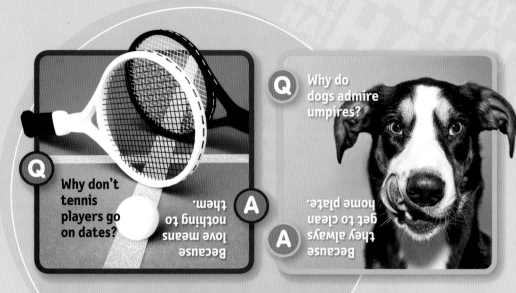

Q Why do dogs admire umpires?

A Because they always get to clean home plate.

Q Why did the cyclist prefer riding a unicycle?

A She just couldn't handlebars.

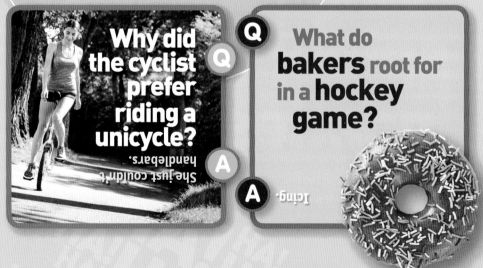

Q What do **bakers** root for in a **hockey game?**

A Icing.

KNOCK,

KNOCK.

Who's there?
Snail.
Snail who?
Snail the pitch,
slug-ger.

A recently discovered snail native to southern China, the smallest ever found, can fit in the eye of a needle!

When light hits a chameleon's skin, the cells appear different colors depending on the animal's mood.

Q What **foul** did the **octopus commit** in the basketball game?

A Octuple dribble.

Q Did you hear about the giraffes who raced each other?

A They were neck and neck the whole way.

106

KNOCK, KNOCK.

Who's there?
Island.
Island who?
Island on all fours after losing my footing.

A group of kittens is called a kindle.

107

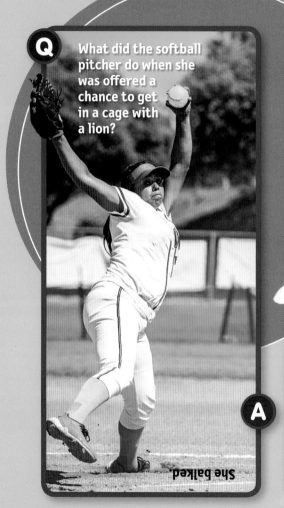

Q What did the softball pitcher do when she was offered a chance to get in a cage with a lion?

A

She balked.

Q What new sport would a hive of bees love to watch?

A

Drone racing!

Q What is a **caterpillar's** favorite **sport?**

A Curling.

Say this fast three times:

The **hoarse horse** rehearsed the course.

Q What is a penguin's favorite part of a football game?

A When they ice the kicker.

Q Why do tiger families always root for rookies?

A They like to see them earn their stripes.

GO TEAM

KNOCK, KNOCK.

Who's there?
Meow.
Meow who?
Take meow to the ball game ...

Cats can't taste sweetness.

Where does a comic book hero like to watch sports?

The Superdome.

A

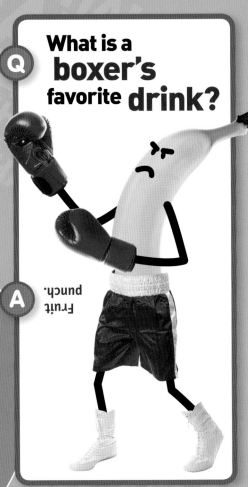

Q

What is a boxer's favorite drink?

A

Fruit punch.

114

SPORTS TEAMS JUST LOVE NAMING THEMSELVES AFTER ME!

ANIMAL: Golden eagle
NAME: Edie
FAVORITE SPORT: High diving
FAVORITE SPORTS PLAY:
When the team in the lead swoops in for the kill

Fierce FANS

115

SPECTACULAR SPORT:
Tapati Rapa Nui

LOCATION: Easter Island

SURPRISING STATS:

You might know Easter Island (also called Rapa Nui) for its 887 moai—giant statues carved from volcanic rock. However, Easter Island is also home to another amazing feat: Tapati Rapa Nui, a festival of celebrations and competitive sports events. Tapati Rapa Nui began in the 1970s as an homage to Easter Island's unique history and culture, and culminates with the crowning of that year's Queen of Tapati. Celebrations feature horse racing, dance competitions, traditional sporting events, and an island triathlon. The most famous event is the Haka Pei, in which contestants in loincloths slide down the slope of a 985 foot (300 m) volcano on banana tree trunks.

Participants in the Haka Pei can reach speeds up to 50 miles an hour (80 km/h).

Easter Island, a territory of Chile, is 1,200 miles (1,931 km) from the nearest landmass.

Super Cool Sports

Q What do dogs root for in baseball?

A A walk.

Q What gymnastic event do barnyard animals like most?

A The pommel horse.

Q Why did the chess master have to borrow his pieces?

A He pawned all his sets.

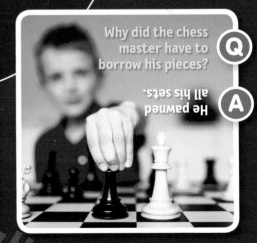

Chickens have at least 24 different calls.

KNOCK, KNOCK.
Who's there?
Lacrosse.
Lacrosse who?
Lacrosse the street quickly and get to the park!

WHENEVER SKI JUMPERS NEED A SPOTTER, THEY ALWAYS ASK ME FIRST!

Sports TALK

Q Where do cows warm up for a baseball game?

A The bull pen.

Q Where do dogs most like to watch a game?

A The woof.

Q Where does a groundhog like to sit during a baseball game?

A The dugout.

Q What did the **baseball** player order for **dessert?**

A Bundt cake.

KNOCK, KNOCK.

Who's there?
Paddle.
Paddle who?
Paddle open the door soon if you give her a second!

Beavers use their paddle-shaped tail like a rudder and are graceful swimmers.

123

I TRY NOT TO PLAY TOO RUFF!

ANIMAL: Bulldog

NAME: Bonnie

FAVORITE SPORT: Basketball

FAVORITE SPORTS PLAY: When the players dribble all over the floor

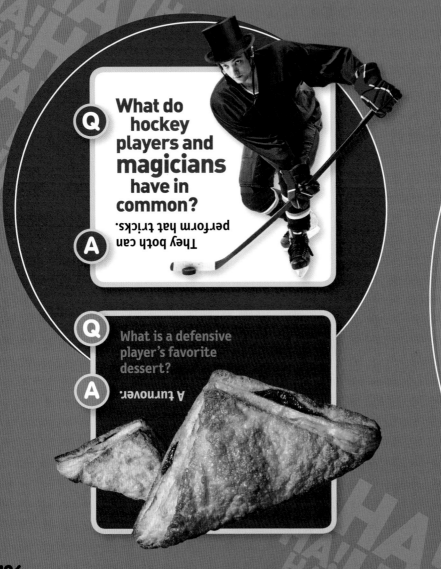

Q What do hockey players and **magicians** have in common?

A They both can perform hat tricks.

Q What is a defensive player's favorite dessert?

A A turnover.

127

129

ASA: What do you do when you see a buffalo with a basketball?
KEITH: Try to block her?
ASA: No, you get out of the way!

A weatherman's favorite sports teams:

- Tampa Bay Lightning
- Oklahoma City Thunder
- Miami Heat
- Phoenix Suns
- Carolina Hurricanes

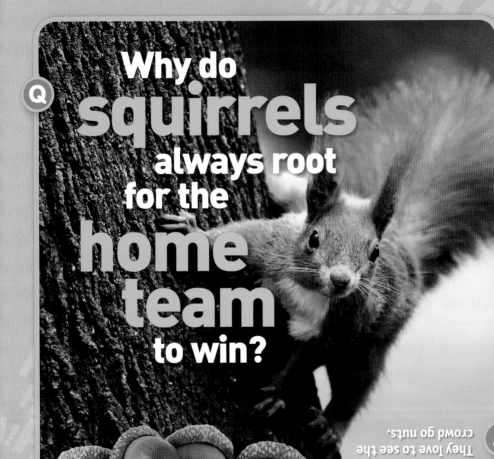

Q Why do **squirrels** always root for the **home team** to win?

A They love to see the crowd go nuts.

131

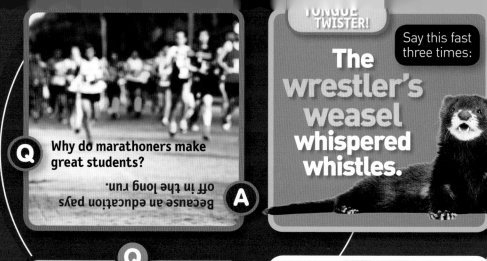

Q Why do marathoners make great students?

A Because an education pays off in the long run.

Say this fast three times:

The wrestler's weasel whispered whistles.

Q Who did the **cyclist** ask to repair her wheel?

A The spokesperson.

Q Why were the tennis players grounded?

A For making too much of a racket.

The term "home plate" probably refers to the iron disks that were used for baseball games in the 1800s.

KNOCK, KNOCK.

Who's there?
Meow.
Meow who?
Meow at home plate after the catcher tagged me.

Q

What type of **dinosaur** loves **motorsports racing?**

Veloci-raptors!

Ⓐ

Q Why did all the commuters steer clear of the bicyclist?

A They heard she's a cycle-path.

Sports TALK

I JUST LOVE THE SEVENTH-INNING STRETCH.

136

African elephants use tusks to dig for food and water and strip bark from trees.

KNOCK, KNOCK.

Who's there?
Dewey.
Dewey who?
Dewey have enough time to get peanuts and snacks before the game starts?

137

Super Cool ★★
★ Sports

Lumberjack World Championships

LOCATION: Hayward, WI, U.S.A.

SURPRISING STATS:

You've probably heard of lumberjacks, but have you heard of the Lumberjack World Championships? Logging—harvesting and transporting trees—has been around for thousands of years, but it wasn't until 1960 that the first Lumberjack World Championship was held to showcase the incredible athleticism it takes to be a logger. The championship now showcases more than 20 traditional timber sport skills for men and women, including logrolling, pole climbing, and wood chopping and sawing. One of the most popular events is known as logrolling: Two competitors balance at either end of a log and sprint, kick, and roll the log in order to knock each other off and into the cold water below!

One Lumberjack World Championship event requires contestants to climb a 90 foot (27 m) tree!

Competitors can win more than $50,000.

139

Q What's black and white and red all over?

A A referee who made a bad call.

Q Why was the basketball court slippery?

CAUTION
WET FLOOR
CAUTION

A The players dribbled all over it.

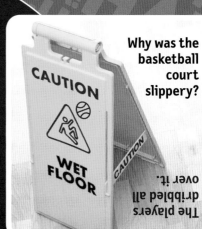

Q Why couldn't the golfer sleep at night?

A She was afraid of the bogeyman.

Q What are a **frog's** two favorite **track and field** events?

A The long jump and high jump.

I'M ALSO GREAT AT COMPETITIVE EATING!

ANIMAL: Polar bear

NAME: Paulie

FAVORITE SPORT: Swimming; fishing

FAVORITE SPORTS PLAY: Seeing an ice hockey goalie freeze the puck

Fierce FANS

Like humans, chimps communicate with facial expressions, gestures, and sounds.

Q

Why are chimps happy to see bad calls during a baseball game?

A They like to see a
manager go bananas.

143

Q What type of tournament do **bird lovers** like most?

A A round robin.

Q Why was the golfer uncomfortable?

A He played with multiple wedgies.

144

Siberian (or Amur) tigers are the world's largest cats.

KNOCK, KNOCK.

Who's there?
Phelps.
Phelps who?
Phelps me get out of the pool?

145

TONGUE TWISTER!

Say this fast three times:

The fish secretly wished for a swish.

Q Why were the elephants tossed out of the swimming pool?

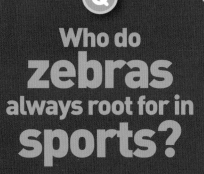

A They wouldn't keep their trunks up.

Q What type of cheese do experienced athletes like best?

A Pro-volone.

Q Who do **zebras** always root for in **sports?**

A The referees.

146

147

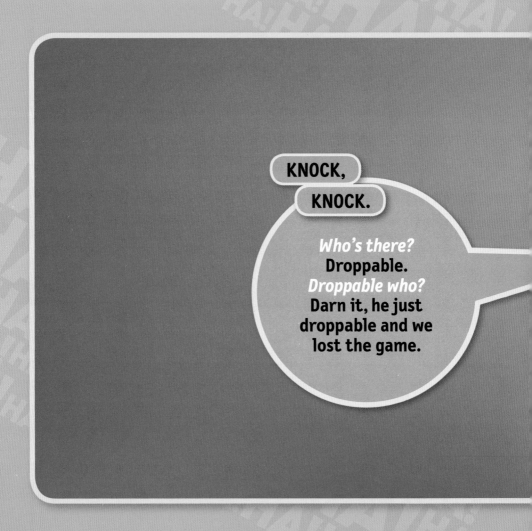

Q What type of
noisy cattle
show up at
sporting events?

A Cow-bells.

Q What is
a mule's
favorite
sport?

A Kickball.

Q How does a
football player
carry his
groceries?

A In a
quarterback
sack.

Q What **baseball**
position would a
**young
vampire**
have?

A Batboy.

Q

What did the

elephant

say when
his favorite team
lost the World Series?

A "Tusk, tusk."

151

Q

What do you call an
all-owl
tailgate party?

Owls use their powerful talons to carry animals several times heavier than themselves.

GO TEAM

A hootenanny! Ⓐ

153

DOES THIS MEAN I MADE BIRDIE?

Sports TALK

Q Why do **tennis players** make great **tea party hosts?**

A They're really good at serving.

Q What is a **goat's** favorite part of a bicycle race?

A The mountain stages.

Q What do bad teams and puppies have in common?

A They like to roll over when it gets late.

Because pigeons are so used to humans and dense urban areas, they will sometimes land on a field during play and delay the game!

KNOCK, KNOCK.

Who's there?
Pigeon.
Pigeon who?
Pigeon and swingin'—
that's baseball
for ya!

Why couldn't the snowboarder fix the leaky sink?

She only used a half-pipe.

Q Where did the **janitor bat** in the **lineup?**

A Cleanup.

Q What's the martial artist's favorite drink?

A Kara-tea.

Q

Why did the
player
leap into
the group
of fans?

She needed to cool off!

A

TONGUE TWISTER!

Say this fast three times:

Hockey jocks rock crazy socks.

Q **Why did the quarterback's car get towed?**

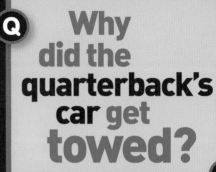

A He parked in the Red Zone.

Q What did the trainer tell the owners of a seafood restaurant?

A "You need more mussels."

Q **Why was the bowler confused by baseball?**

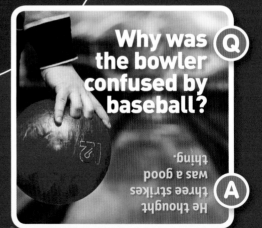

A He thought three strikes was a good thing.

164

Leopard seals stay warm with a thick layer of fat known as blubber.

165

Why do kittens and puppies like when one team takes **a big lead** early in a game?

Q

A

Because they love to watch the other team claw back.

167

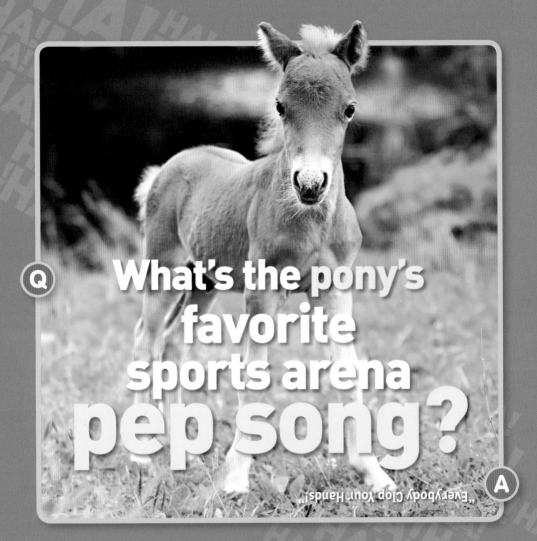

Q What's the pony's favorite sports arena pep song?

A "Everybody Clop Your Hands!"

168

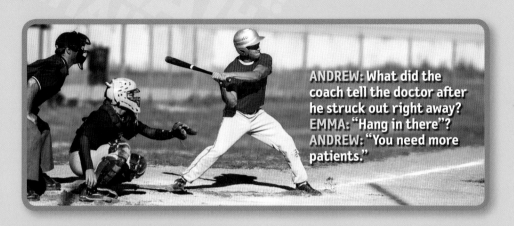

ANDREW: What did the coach tell the doctor after he struck out right away?
EMMA: "Hang in there"?
ANDREW: "You need more patients."

Biggest fans of the Orlando Magic:

- Wizards
- Witches
- Sorcerers
- Houdini
- Carpets

169

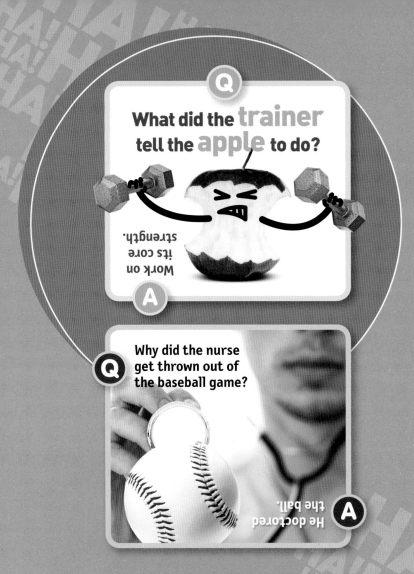

Q

What did the **trainer** tell the **apple** to do?

A Work on its core strength.

Q Why did the nurse get thrown out of the baseball game?

A He doctored the ball.

170

Some seal pups are weaned in only 10 to 12 days, during which time their mass doubles.

KNOCK, KNOCK.

Who's there?
Spy kit.
Spy kit who?
If you won't try to spy kit, we can't win the volleyball game!

What breed of dog is the best at football?

Golden receivers.

A

Did you hear about the new **Q**
baseball-themed sci-fi movie?

A It's called
*The Umpire
Strikes Back.*

Baseball matchups that should never occur in nature:

- Cubs vs. Cardinals
- Tigers vs. Orioles
- Blue Jays vs. Diamondbacks
- Mariners vs. Rockies

Q Why did the barber get called out of bounds?

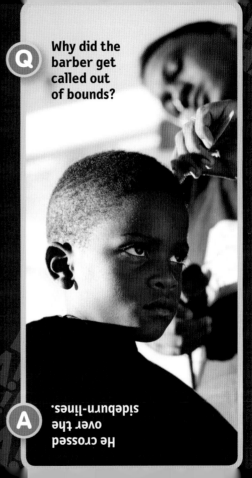

A He crossed over the sideburn-lines.

Q What did the punt returner order from the seafood restaurant?

A The fair catch of the day.

TONGUE TWISTER!

Say this fast three times:

The slick SOW did a triple salchow.

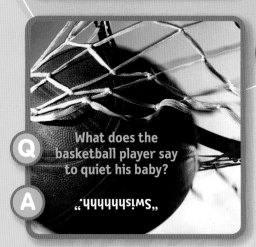

Q What does the basketball player say to quiet his baby?

A "Swishhhhhh."

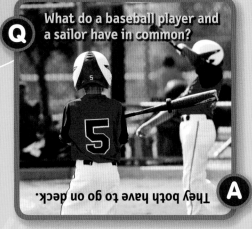

Q What do a baseball player and a sailor have in common?

A They both have to go on deck.

KNOCK, KNOCK.

Who's there?
Gopher.
Gopher who?
Let's gopher a swim!

Gophers' cheek pouches are used for carrying plant food they find when burrowing underground.

Leopards often hunt from trees, where their spotted coats allow them to blend with the leaves.

Why did the leopard arrive early to the game?

Because he wanted to find good spots.

Q Why did the diving team disband?

A They had a falling-out.

Q What do **farmers markets** and **college football** have in common?

A They both have peach, orange, and rose bowls.

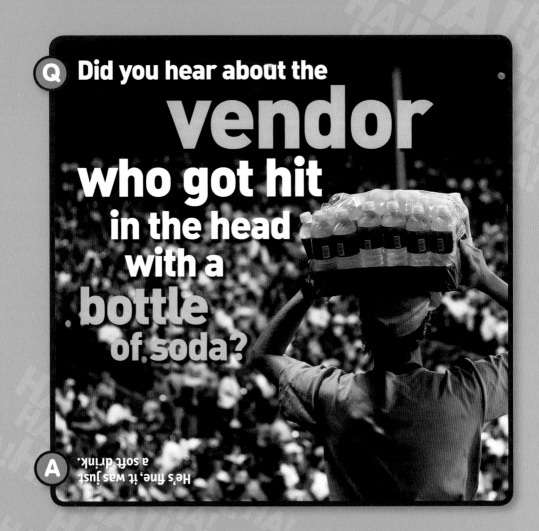

Q Did you hear about the **vendor** who got hit in the head with a **bottle** of soda?

A He's fine, it was just a soft drink.

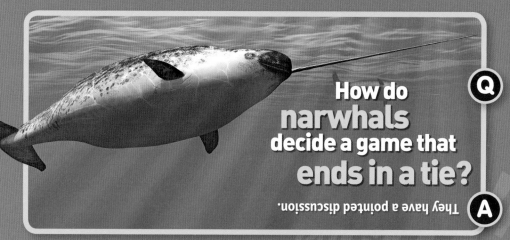

Q How do **narwhals** decide a game that ends in a tie?

A They have a pointed discussion.

Football matchups that should never occur in nature:

- Bears vs. Cardinals
- Lions vs. Seahawks
- Bengals vs. Rams
- Jaguars vs. Dolphins
- Broncos vs. Falcons

Q What was the hockey player's favorite **holiday** song?

A "0, Goalie Night."

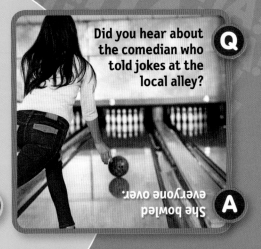

Q Did you hear about the comedian who told jokes at the local alley?

A She bowled everyone over.

Q What is a fisherman's favorite pitch?

A The sinker.

Q What is a swimmer's second favorite sport?

A Pool.

Under their fur, polar bears have black skin.

Q **What is a sheep's favorite sport?**

Baasket baaall.

Say this fast three times:

The orangutan flashed his furious fangs.

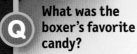

What was the boxer's favorite candy?

Q

A sucker punch.

A

Why are zombies good at sports interviews?

They always give good sound bites.

Say this fast three times:

Goalies grow glowing colts.

Q Why is a comedian good at making baseballs?

A He can put them in stitches.

Q Why couldn't the players leave the locker room?

A Their coach called a team timeout.

Q How did the candle get through the sports season?

A He took it one match at a time.

Some woodpeckers can peck holes so large in trees that they can cause the trees to break in half.

SPECTACULAR SPORT:
Iditarod

LOCATION: Alaska, U.S.A.

SURPRISING STATS:

Although the Iditarod of today is a world-famous event, it actually grew out of practical purposes. In days when snowmobiles were either too undependable or nonexistent, inhabitants of Alaska relied on their faithful sled dogs for transportation, hauling gold, and delivering mail and food. The most common of these routes was from Seward to Nome. In 1973, after snowmobiles began to overtake sled dog travel in popularity, the Iditarod was founded to preserve sled dog culture and the mighty Alaskan huskies. Today, contestants lead teams of huskies on a 975-mile (1,569-km) race along the historic Iditarod Trail.

Today's mushers usually complete the trail in 9 to 12 days. The same journey in the early 1900s would have taken weeks or months.

In 1925, a team of sled dogs ran the Iditarod to deliver a lifesaving medicine to the children of Nome, who suffered from influenza.

194

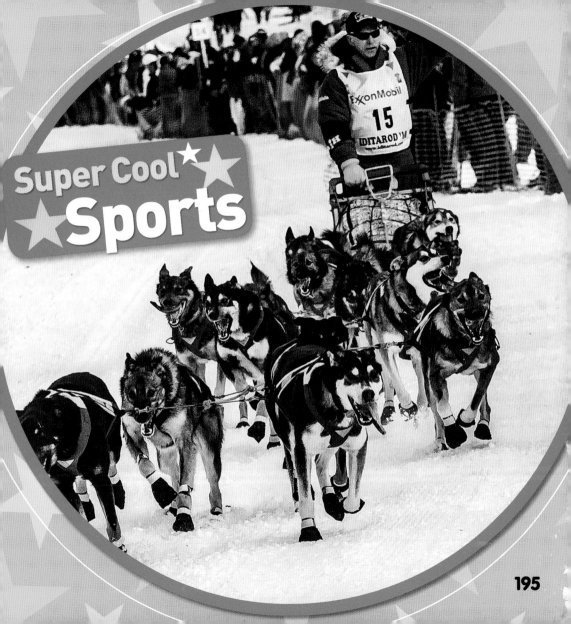

Super Cool
Sports

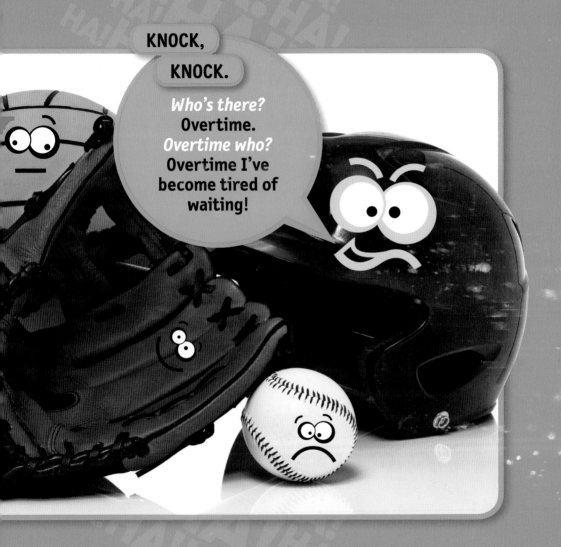

JOSE: Do you know why the soccer players were scared of the *T. rex* on the opposing team?
MICHELLE: Because they were worried he might eat them?
JOSE: No, because he always dino-scored!

Q **Why did the soccer coach flood the pitch?**

He wanted to bring on the sub. **A**

Crocodile encounters on golf courses can be common in places with a tropical climate.

KNOCK, KNOCK.

Who's there?
Wooden shoe.
Wooden shoe who?
Wooden shoe like to play a round of golf?

201

JOKEFINDER

ILLUSTRATION CREDITS

Credit Abbreviations:
DS = Dreamstime; GI = Getty Images; IS = iStockphoto;
SS = Shutterstock

Front cover and spine: Javier Brosch/SS; **back cover:** (dog), ane-tapics/SS;(masks), Sean Locke photography/SS;(carrot), Marina Sliusarenko/SS; 4–5, Geoffrey Kuchera/DS; 6, Eagleflying/DS; 7 (UP RT), Aagje De Jong/DS; 7 (CTR RT), mTaira/SS; 8 (UP RT), Imagecom/DS; 8 (ball), Magdalena urawska/DS; 8 (UP LE), Joseph Sohm/SS; 8 (hornet), irin-k/SS; 8 (LO LE), Blend Images/SS; 9, Paulus Rusyanto/DS; 10 (UP LE), Fabian Schmidt/DS; 10 (LO LE), Pixattitude/DS; 10 (ice rink), vkilikov/SS; 10 (skates), Inhabitant/SS; 10 (mouse), Rudmer Zwerver/DS; 11, Jacoba Susanna Maria Swanepoel/DS; 11 (racquet), Michael Pettigrew/SS; 12 (UP LE), Pyshnyy Maxim Vjacheslavovich/SS; 12 (LO RT), Jerry Zitterman/SS; 12 (UP RT), ARENA Creative/SS; 12 (cookie), Tracy Decourcy/DS; 12 (LO LE), Dudarev Mikhail/SS; 13, Michael C. Gray/SS; 14–15, 2630ben/SS; 15 (helmet), pbombaert/SS; 16 (UP), Sinnerga/DS; 16 (LO), Dasha Petrenko/SS; 17 (CTR), teekayu/SS; 17 (sweatband), t_kimura/IS/GI; 18 (UP LE), NGS Image Collection; 18 (UP RT), Iurii Osadchi/SS; 18 (ball), Daniel Thornberg/DS; 18 (LO LE), 4x6/IS/GI; 18 (LO RT), Alvov/SS; 19, stask/IS/GI; 20–21 (CTR LE), Eti Swinford/DS; 21 (LO CTR), KAMONRAT/SS; 21 (UP CTR), Marina Sliusarenko/SS; 21 (belt), alaa/SS; 22–23 (CTR), Sudpoth Sirirattanasakul/SS; 23 (LO CTR), Collinjloveless/DS; 24 (UP RT), nikkytok/SS; 24 (LO RT), dny3d/SS; 24 (LO LE), Igor Zakowski/SS; 24 (skateboard), Panda Vector/SS; 24 (UP LE), Inked Pixels/SS; 24 (baseball glove), Nor Gal/SS; 25, lunatic67/SS; 25 (hat), Etaphop photo/SS; 26 (LO RT), Valentina Razumova/SS; 27 (CTR), a katz/SS; 28–29 (CTR RT), Joewarut/DS; 28–29 (LO CTR RT), Mtsaride/SS; 30 (UP LE), Willeecole/DS; 30 (LO LE), bluehand/SS; 30–31 (CTR RT), Phil Mcdonald/DS; 32, Adam Van Spronsen/SS; 33 (RT), Tetiana Kozachok/DS; 33 (LE), Michael Valos/DS; 33 (pennant), Mike Flippo/SS; 34 (UP RT), sirtravelalot/SS; 34 (fence), inxti/SS; 34 (cartoon eyes), igor malovic/SS; 34 (LO RT), sirtravelalot/SS; 34 (volleyball), worananphoto/SS; 34 (UP LE), GMEVIPHOTO/SS; 34 (cartoon mouth), Val_Zar/SS; 35, Shevs/SS; 36 (koalas), Eric Isselee/SS; 36 (LO), Mark Herreid/SS; 36 (UP), eastern light photography/SS; 36 (football), Mtsaride/SS; 36–37 (CTR RT), mooinblack/SS; 38–39 (LO RT), Michael Flippo/DS; 38 (LO CTR), fivespots/SS; 39 (CTR), GeorgePeters/IS/GI; 40 (UP), Valeria Cantone/DS; 40 (LO), Nicole Hollenstein/SS; 40–41 (CTR RT), SphaeraDesigns/SS; 42 (UP), SantiPhotoSS/SS; 42 (LO), Yuganov Konstantin/SS; 43 (RT), Dvo/SS; 43 (CTR LE), Lucia Fox/SS; 44–45, Curioso Travel Photography/BigStock.com; 44–45 (toy car), Pattarapong Kumlert/DS; 46 (LO RT), Anke Van Wyk/DS; 46 (LO LE), Torsak/DS; 46 (UP RT), Duplass/SS; 46 (UP LE), Ewais/SS; 46 (bee), irin–k/SS; 47 (turkey), veleknez/SS; 47, AS photo studio/SS; 48 (baseball), Willard/IS/GI; 48 (RT), Paul Michael Hughes/SS; 48 (microphone), rangizzz/SS; 49 (CTR), anetapics/SS; 49 (mask), Sean Locke Photography/SS; 50 (CTR), rujithai/SS; 51 (CTR RT), Dewi Putra/SS; 51 (LO RT), Surin Phumphuang 1/SS; 51 (UP RT), CamBuff/SS; 52–53, Rtrembly/DS; 53 (rhino), Gualtiero Boffi/DS; 54 (LO RT), Arne9001/DS; 54 (pirate hat), GillianVann/SS; 54 (baseball), Dan Thornberg/SS; 54 (UP LE), Callipso/SS; 55, Rob Hainer/SS; 56, KPG_Payless/SS; 57 (UP), Brand X; 57 (LO), Eric Isselee/SS; 58–59, Johan Swanepoel/SS; 60 (LO), alexei_tm/SS; 60 (UP), Oleg Bezrukov/SS; 60–61 (CTR RT), red–feniks/SS; 62 (UP RT), Yobro10/DS; 62 (chicken), Aksenova Natalya/SS; 62 (LO LE), Ksenia Merenkova/SS; 62 (baseball), Dan Thornberg/SS; 62 (UP LE), Yana Mavlyutova/SS; 63 (CTR), Digital Storm/SS; 63 (shoes), Etaphop photo/SS; 64–65, sirtravelalot/SS; 66 (RT), CTRPhotos/IS/GI; 66 (basketball), Lightspring/SS; 66 (LE), photomaster/SS; 67 (pie), Brand X; 67 (CTR), JoeLena/IS/GI; 68–69 (CTR), asiseeit/IS/GI; 69 (feather pen), viktoriya89/BigStock.com; 70 (LO LE), Samantha Reinders; 70 (UP LE), Matimix/DS; 70 (LO RT), EpicStockMedia/SS; 70 (UP RT), Steve Lovegrove/SS; 71 (CTR), Daniel Thornberg/DS; 72 (LO RT), Irina Kovancova/SS; 72 (UP RT), leoks/SS; 72 (CTR RT), M. Rohana/SS; 73 (CTR), M. Rohana/SS; 74 (LO LE), Stock Up/SS; 74 (UP LE), Tomnamon/SS; 74–75 (CTR RT), szefei/SS; 75 (ketchup), Sanit Fuangnakhon/SS; 76–77, Luiz Felipe V. Puntel/SS; 78 (UP RT), BilevichOlga/IS/GI; 78 (UP LE), Four Oaks/SS; 78 (baseball bat), CrackerClips Stock Media/SS; 78 (snowy hill), calmmindphoto/SS; 78 (LO RT), Rosa Jay/SS; 79, Solomiya Malovana/SS; 80 (LO), Steve Debenport/IS/GI; 80 (UP), Randy Rimland/SS; 81, Independent birds/SS; 81 (stopwatch), rangizzz/SS; 82, Eric Cote/SS; 83 (RT), weerapatkiatdumrong/IS/GI; 83 (LE), 3523studio/SS; 84–85, picsbyst/SS; 84–85 (candy), Texturis/SS; 86 (laptop), Lasse Kristensen/DS; 86 (hot dog), Valentina Razumova/DS; 86 (LO RT), vlad09/SS; 86 (LE), mTaira/SS; 87 (LO LE), Shevelartur/DS; 87 (golf ball), Photodisc; 87 (RT), eyeCatch-Light Photography/SS; 87 (UP LE), Colin Edwards Wildside/SS; 88 (UP LE), clearviewstock/SS; 88 (LO RT), Ultrashock/SS; 88 (goggles), Mega Pixel/SS; 88 (UP RT), Svietlieisha Olena/SS; 88 (red cap), Etaphop photo/SS; 89 (CTR), boynatural/IS/GI; 90, Hintau Aliaksei/SS; 91 (UP), Serrnovik/DS; 91 (LO), cinoby/IS/GI; 92–93, Zeiss4Me/IS/GI; 94 (CTR), Xinhua/Alamy Stock Photo; 95 (LO RT), Xinhua/Alamy Stock Photo; 95 (UP RT), Wendy White/Alamy Stock Photo; 96 (LO LE), Richard Brosseau/DS; 96 (LO RT), ruthrose/IS/GI; 96 (UP LE), yuran-78/IS/GI; 96 (pirate hook), anusorn nakdee/IS/GI; 96 (beetle), Eric Isselee/SS; 96 (UP RT), Aaron Amat/SS; 97, Alantunnicliffe/DS; 98–99, Gudkov Andrey/SS; 100 (LO LE), Vishnevskiy Vasily/SS; 100 (basketball), Lightspring/SS; 100 (UP), iurii/SS; 100 (bat), Mega Pixel/SS; 101 (spider), iSKYDANCER/SS; 101 (CTR), William G Carpenter/SS; 102 (LO RT), Demkat/SS; 102 (UP LE), Olga Sabarova/DS; 102 (UP RT), Amy Rene/SS; 102 (LO LE), nullplus/SS; 103, Jjustas/SS; 104–105, taboga/SS; 104 (baseball mitt), Sergiy1975/SS; 104 (UP RT), Etaphop photo/SS; 106 (LO LE), Martin Novak/SS; 106 (basketball), Lightspring/SS; 106 (UP CTR), Yellow Cat/SS; 106–107 (CTR RT), S7chvetik/DS; 108 (RT), Chesky/SS; 108 (bee), Vinicius Tupinamba/SS; 108 (LE), Jon Osumi/SS; 109, Ingrid Curry/SS; 110 (football), Michael Flippo/DS; 110 (LO LE), Jan Martin Will/SS; 110 (LO RT), Stayer/SS; 110 (pennant), Mike Flippo/SS; 110 (UP RT), Sari 0Neal/SS; 110 (UP LE), Niney Azman/SS; 111 (CTR), AP Photo/Bill Fundaro; 112–113, Adya/SS; 114 (LE), David Mcshane/DS; 114 (banana), Bjørn Hovdal/DS; 114 (shorts/boots), Nicholas Piccillo/SS; 114 (superhero), Alexandra Petruk/SS; 114 (boxing gloves), xmee/SS; 115 (CTR), davemhuntphotography/SS; 116 (UP CTR RT), Viktor Gmyria/DS; 116 (LO CTR RT), Svetlana Prochazkova/DS; 117 (CTR), T photography/SS; 118 (goat), cs333/SS; 118 (UP LE), Javier Brosch/SS; 118 (UP RT), Danilovski/SS; 118 (LO RT), Mikkel Bigandt/SS; 119 (lacrosse stick), Trinacria Photo/SS; 119, Grigorita Ko/SS; 120–121, Abeselom Zerit/SS; 122 (LO RT), Brand X; 122 (UP LE), Christopher Bies/DS; 122 (marmot), Vladimir Melnik/SS; 122 (LO LE), David Lee/SS; 122 (UP RT), Tami Freed/SS; 123, Daniel Rose/SS; 124–125 (CTR LE), ruthrose/IS/GI; 125 (LO LE), WilleeCole Photography/SS; 126 (LO), Brand X; 126 (UP), Michael Pettigrew/DS; 126 (hat), Gjermund/SS; 126–127 (CTR RT), sirtravelalot/SS; 128–129, Debbie Steinhausser/SS; 130 (LO), yev-geniy11/SS; 130 (UP), J Reineke/SS; 130 (basketball), Aaron Amat/SS; 131 (CTR), seawhisper/SS; 131 (CTR LE), AS Food studio/SS; 132 (LO LE), Ilya Andriyanov/SS; 132 (LO RT), sirtravelalot/SS; 132 (UP RT), Inna Astakhova/SS; 132 (UP LE), Alextype/SS; 133, Shane Morris/DS; 133 (cat), skodonnell/IS/GI; 134–135 (CTR), Cheng Wei/SS; 135 (flag), Photodisc; 136 (UP), Serrnovik/DS; 136 (LO), Brocreative/SS; 136–137 (CTR RT), Mark Atkins/SS; 138 (CTR), Brett Morgan Photography; 139 (chainsawing), Aperture by Steve Davis; 139 (pole climbing), Aperture by Steve Davis; 139 (sawing), Aperture by Steve Davis; 140 (UP LE), Brand X; 140 (UP RT), shank_ali/IS/GI; 140 (LO RT), Robynrg/SS; 140 (LO LE), Albe84/SS; 141, Iakov Filimonov/SS; 142–143, Sergey Uryadnikov/SS; 142–143 (hats), Grafner/DS; 144 (LO), Siraphol/DS; 144 (UP), Brian Guest/SS; 144 (golf clubs), Dan Thornberg/SS; 144–145 (CTR RT), nattanan726/SS; 145 (CTR RT), Indigolotos/DS; 146 (UP LE), Matt Propert; 146 (UP RT), Photodisc; 146 (LO LE), Luca Santilli/SS; 146 (trophy), Chones/SS; 147, Chris Howey/SS; 148–149 (CTR), shironosov/IS/GI; 150 (UP RT), Neil Lockhart/DS; 150 (grocery bag), Gino Santa Maria/SS; 150 (LO LE), ostill/SS; 150 (UP LE), Astrid Gast/SS; 150 (LO RT), siridhata/SS; 151, Mark O'Flaherty/SS; 152–153, Tathoms/SS; 153 (CTR RT), Mike Flippo/SS; 153 (CTR LE), Charles Brutlag, 154 (UP), jhorrocks/IS/GI; 154 (tennis ball), Zheltyshev/SS; 155, Maria Komar/SS; 155 (CTR), Gerry Ellis/Digital Vision; 156 (LO), Onetouchspark/DS; 156 (UP), Empipe/DS; 156–157 (CTR RT), TriggerPhoto/IS/GI; 156–157 (pigeon), Huaykwang/SS; 158–158 (wrench), Michael Flippo/DS; 158–159, Zaretska Olga/SS; 160 (RT), 0STILL/IS/GI; 160 (tea cup), artjazz/SS; 160 (broom), Keith Publicover/SS; 160 (LE), Kaderov Andrii/SS; 161 (CTR), Grigorita Ko/SS; 162 (LO LE), Eric Isselee/SS; 162 (CTR), Shooter Bob Square Lenses/SS; 163, Max Topchii/SS; 164 (UP LE), Corepics Vof/DS; 164 (LO LE), margouillat photo/SS; 164 (LO RT), AS photo studio/SS; 165, Dmytro Pylypenko/SS; 166–167, Happy monkey/SS; 167 (UP RT), Brocreative/SS; 168 (CTR), DragoNika/SS; 169 (LO), Pikoso.kz/SS; 169 (basketball), Lightspring/SS; 169 (UP), Billion Photos/SS; 170 (UP CTR), Timothy Geiss/SS; 170 (apple), Jeeragone Inrut/DS; 170 (LO), Andrei Rahalski/DS; 170 (baseball), Tomislav Forgo/SS; 170–171 (CTR RT), David Osborn/SS; 172–173, ESB Professional/SS; 173 (LO CTR), Michael Flippo/DS; 174 (CTR), Kent Weakley/SS; 175 (RT), rez-art/IS/GI; 175 (bluejay), Mike Truchon/SS; 175 (snake), Eric Isselee/SS; 176 (UP LE), holbox/SS; 176 (LO LE), JoffreyM/SS; 176 (football), Mtsaride/SS; 176 (UP RT), photomaster/SS; 176 (skates), Vereshchagin Dmitry/SS; 176 (LO RT), tammykayphoto/SS; 177 (LO RT), Etaphop photo/SS; 177 (gopher), BillieBonsor/SS; 178–179, Stu Porter/DS; 180 (LO), Teri Virbickis/SS; 180 (UP), Yelena Rodriguez/DS; 180–181 (CTR RT), SensorSpot/IS/GI; 182 (CTR), Joy Brown/SS; 183 (sheep), Eric Isselee/SS; 183 (UP), Linda Bucklin/SS; 183 (tiger), apple2499/SS; 184 (LO LE), Arne9001/DS; 184 (LO RT), Red Tiger/SS; 184 (UP RT), Nestor Rizhniak/SS; 184 (UP LE), Longchalerm Rungruang/SS; 185, Susan Sheldon/DS; 186–187, Richard Seeley/SS; 188 (Lollipop), Ruth Black/SS; 188 (LO CTR), On and On/SS; 188–189 (CTR RT), fvtrop/IS/GI; 190–191, Viktor Petrovich/SS; 192 (LO LE), Beto Chagas/SS; 192 (UP RT), mTaira/SS; 192 (LO RT), Gladkiy Nikita/SS; 193 (CTR), Steve Byland/SS; 194 (dogs), AP Photo/Jay Christensen; 194 (dog sled), AP Photo/Eric Engman; 195 (CTR), Troutnut/SS; 196–197, ohmygouche/Getty Images; 196–197 (CTR), Raja Rc/DS; 196–197 (CTR), Raja Rc/DS; 198 (LO), Jeff Thrower/SS; 198 (UP), DM7/SS; 199, Filipe Frazao/SS; 200–201, stevecoleimages/IS/GI; 205, picsbyst/SS

Published by National Geographic Partners, LLC. All rights reserved. Reproduction of the whole or any part of the contents without written permission from the publisher is prohibited.

Since 1888, the National Geographic Society has funded more than 12,000 research, exploration, and preservation projects around the world. The Society receives funds from National Geographic Partners, LLC, funded in part by your purchase. A portion of the proceeds from this book supports this vital work. To learn more, visit natgeo.com/info.

NATIONAL GEOGRAPHIC and Yellow Border Design are trademarks of the National Geographic Society, used under license.

For more information, visit nationalgeographic.com, call 1-800-647-5463, or write to the following address:

National Geographic Partners
1145 17th Street N.W.
Washington, D.C. 20036-4688 U.S.A.

Visit us online at nationalgeographic.com/books

For librarians and teachers:
ngchildrensbooks.org

More for kids from National Geographic:
natgeokids.com

For information about special discounts for bulk purchases, please contact National Geographic Books Special Sales:
specialsales@natgeo.com

For rights or permissions inquiries, please contact National Geographic Books Subsidiary Rights: bookrights@natgeo.com

Editorial, Design, and Production by Mojo Media

Trade paperback ISBN: 978-1-4263-2979-1
Reinforced library binding ISBN: 978-1-4263-2980-7

The publisher would like to thank Paige Towler, project editor; Callie Broaddus, art director; Sarah J. Mock, photo editor; Molly Reid, production editor; Anne LeongSon and Gus Tello, design production assistants.

Printed in China
17/PPS/1